# The New Baby

FIRST EXPERIENCES

# The New Baby

## BY FRED ROGERS

photographs by Jim Judkis

Penguin Putnam Books for Young Readers

With special thanks to: Nan Earl Newell, Research;
Margaret B. McFarland, Ph.D., Senior Consultant;
the Whiteside family and the Chamberlain family.

Text and photographs copyright © 1985 by Family Communications, Inc.
All rights reserved. This book, or parts thereof, may not be reproduced
in any form without permission in writing from the publisher.
A PaperStar Book, published in 1996 by Penguin Putnam Books for Young Readers,
345 Hudson Street, New York, NY 10014. PaperStar Books is a registered trademark of
The Putnam Berkley Group, Inc. The PaperStar logo is a trademark of The Putnam Berkley
Group, Inc. Originally published in 1985 by G. P. Putnam's Sons.
Published simultaneously in Canada. Manufactured in China
Production Assistance: Margy Whitmer. Book Design by Kathleen Westray.
Library of Congress Cataloging-in-Publication Data
Rogers, Fred. The new baby (Mister Rogers' neighborhood—a first experience book)
Summary: Explains the needs of toddlers faced with a new baby in the family, and some
of the changes and disruptions the baby can cause in the life of an older brother or sister.
1. Infants—Juvenile literature. 2. Brother and sisters—Juvenile literature. {1. Babies.
2. Brothers and sisters.}   I. Judkis, Jim, ill.   II. Title.   III. Series: Rogers, Fred. Mister
Rogers' neighborhood (Television program).   HQ 774.R64   1985   305.23   84-26210
ISBN 978-0-698-11366-4
30  29  28  27  26  25

For a firstborn child, the arrival of a baby brother or sister is almost sure to arouse mixed feelings. Along with all the excitement, suddenly someone else is sharing the attention and love that the firstborn used to have all alone. When a child starts feeling unsure about his or her place in the family, that child sometimes reacts with outbursts of anger, baby talk, and other baby ways.

We can help our firstborns to accept a new baby by assuring them of their own special place in the family—a place that no one else can ever take. We can assure them of our love by making special time for them alone with us and by encouraging them to talk about their feelings. And by helping our firstborns feel active and important in the care of the new baby, we can let them know how proud we are of the many ways they're growing.

—Fred Rogers

When your mom has a baby . . .

that baby is a new person in your family.

If the baby's a girl, she's your sister.
If the baby's a boy, he's your brother.

Is it hard to imagine what your family will be like with a new baby there? Just as you can have plenty of love for both your mom and dad, they can have plenty of love for both you *and* the new baby.

You were once a new baby. You had a special place in your family then—and you still have a special place in your family now. You always will—no matter how many children your mom and dad have.

You help your mom and dad feel good about being parents. They can be proud of the way you're growing and proud of all the things you can do.

They like taking care of you *and* they like taking care of the new baby.

But moms and dads sometimes spend so much time
looking at their new babies and holding them and
making faces at them . . .

that they seem to have less time with you.

When people visit new babies, it's the babies who seem to get most of the attention . . . and lots of presents too.

Sometimes older children even wish they were babies again.

When people are busy with the baby, it can seem like they're always saying, "Wait a minute."

When the baby is sleeping, it can seem like people are always saying, "Be quiet." When you're holding the baby, it can seem like people are always saying, "Be careful."

A person could get very grumpy.

But you can do things when you're mad that
don't hurt you or anybody else.

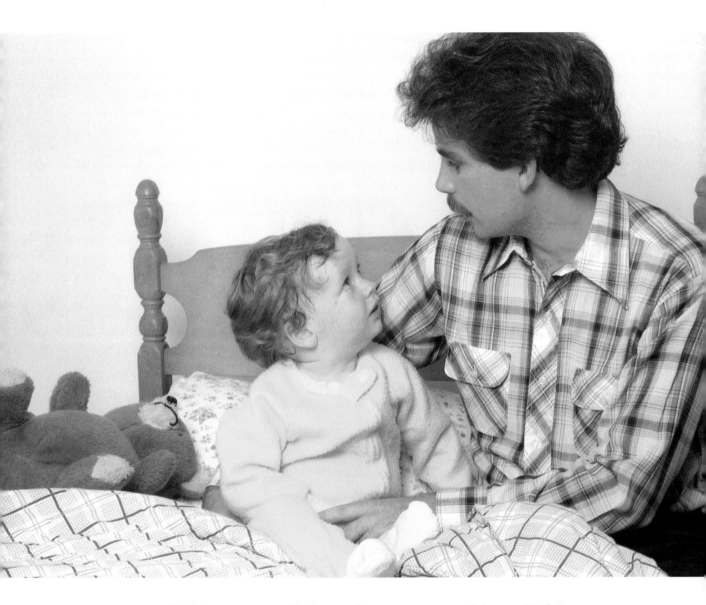

Babies are too little to do very many things. Babies can't talk. You can talk. You can talk about a lot of things . . . even things like how you feel about the new baby in your house.

Babies sleep a lot. They usually sleep in cribs. Did you sleep in a crib when you were very little? Sometimes babies get cribs and clothes and things their big brothers and sisters have grown out of.

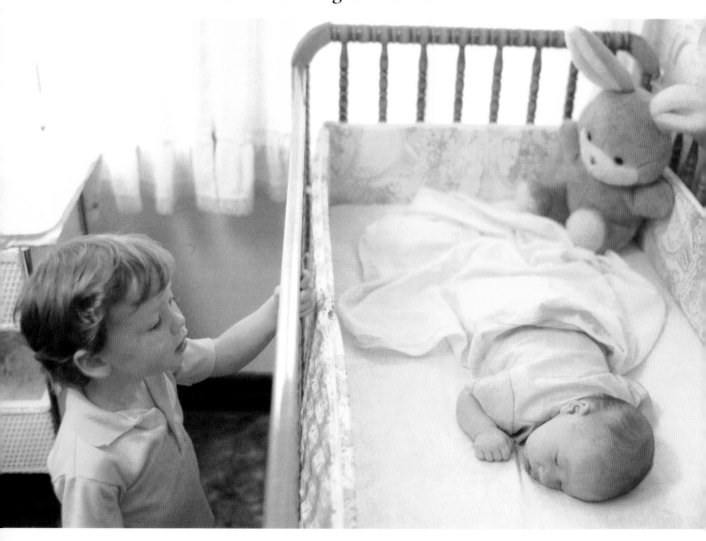

But there are some very important things that a person
shouldn't have to share with anybody.

Babies often get hungry. Sometimes they cry because they don't like to wait to be fed. How is your little brother or sister fed?

It will be a long time before the baby can eat all of the
different things you can eat.

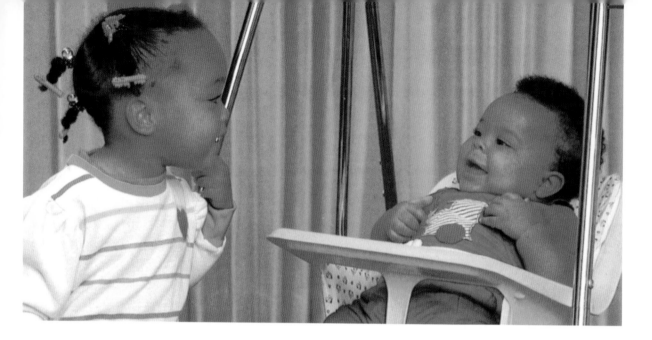

Babies like to listen to your voice and to look at your face.
As you both get older, you can show the baby lots of
things . . . how to smile and laugh . . .

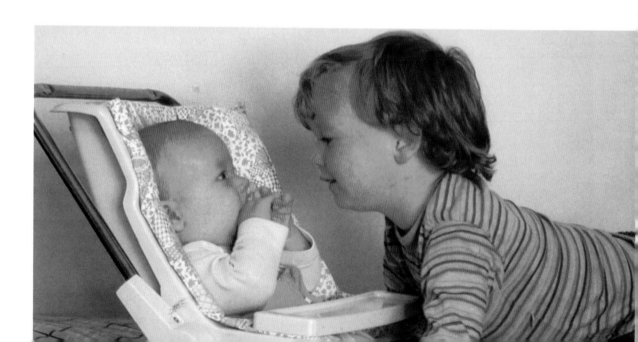

how to play pat-a-cake and peek-a-boo . . .

how to go down a slide . . .

how to draw a picture.

Soon you'll even be able to help the baby
understand about pretending and sharing.

Your new baby needs you for all kinds of times: happy times, sad times and lonely times.

It can make a person feel really good to be needed.

And that's what families are for . . . needing each other
and caring about each other in all kinds of ways.